BABY ANIMALS

HOW TO USE THIS BOOK

Read the captions in the eight-page booklet and, using the labels beside each sticker, choose the image that best fits in the space available.

•

Don't forget that your stickers can be stuck down and peeled off again. If you are careful, you can use your baby animal stickers more than once.

•

You can also use the baby animal stickers to decorate your own books, or for project work at school.

DK

LONDON, NEW YORK, MELBOURNE,
MUNICH, DELHI

First American Edition, 2001
Second American Edition, 2004

08 10 9 8 7

Published in the United States by
DK Publishing, Inc.
375 Hudson Street
New York, New York 10014

Written and edited by Melanie Halton
Designed by Ann Cannings

ISBN-13: 978-0-7566-0564-3

Color reproduction by Reflex Reprographics, UK; Colourscan, Singapore
Printed and bound in China by L. Rex

Dorling Kindersley would like to thank:
Peter Anderson; Jon Bouchier; Paul Bricknell; Geoff Brightling; Jane Burton; Peter Chen; Gordon Clayton; Andy Crawford; Peter Downs; Neil Fletcher; Frank Greenaway; Marc Henrie; Colin Keates; Dave King; Cyril Laubscher; Bill Ling; Nick Parfitt; Tim Ridley; Steve Shott; Kim Taylor; Barrie Watts; and Jerry Young for photography

All other images © Dorling Kindersley.
For further information see www.dkimages.com

Discover more at
www.dk.com

Animal variations

From furry mammals and feathered birds to scaly reptiles and moist-skinned amphibians, thousands of fascinating creatures make up the animal kingdom. All need food to survive, and their diet depends on where they live. Some creatures live alone, others in large communities. While many animals roam around on land, others dwell in ocean waters. The variety of animals makes the world a lively and colorful place.

Long-necked giraffe
A young giraffe is born with the distinctive patterned coat markings of an adult giraffe. When fully grown, giraffes are the tallest animals to walk on land. Their long necks allow them to graze on treetops, which other animals are unable to reach. These hoofed mammals usually live in small herds.

Hoofed horse
This slender-legged foal (baby horse) belongs to an intelligent group of animals – the horse family. Other members include ponies, donkeys, and zebras. They all have only one toe (a hoof) on each foot. Wild horses roam the open countryside in herds. They feed on grasses and plants, and travel great distances to find new grazing land.

Night mice

These furry little mice belong to a group of mammals called rodents. Mice have short gray or brown fur, a long scaly tail, and five toes on each foot. They also have sharp front teeth for cutting food. Most mice are active at night – they have very sensitive whiskers for finding their way in the dark.

Tough-coated rhinoceros
The plant-eating rhinoceros is the biggest land mammal, apart from the elephant. Its large horns, thick skin, and impressive size all help to protect it against enemies. Despite its bulk, a rhino can charge at predators at speeds of up to 30 mph (48 kmh).

Domestic dogs
These playful domestic puppies belong to the dog family. Domestic dogs are kept as pets or work on farms, where they help to herd farm animals. Herding dogs are usually light coloured so they are more visible in bad weather or in the dark.

Grazing cattle
This cute baby calf will grow up to become a large, stocky cow. Members of the cattle family, cows have wide heads and two-toed, hoofed feet. They live in herds and graze on grasses. Cows were first domesticated about 9,000 years ago to provide humans with milk, meat, and leather.

Scary shark

Sharks have survived in the world's oceans for 500 million years. There are more than 400 different species of this fierce-looking animal, from the tiny pygmy shark, to this harmless dogfish, to the gigantic whale shark. Many people believe that sharks eat humans, but in fact most prefer sea creatures such as fish, crabs, seals, and turtles.

Well-adapted reptile

The scaly caiman is related to crocodiles and alligators. This group of reptiles have survived on Earth since the days of the dinosaurs and have changed little since then. Most live in tropical fresh water, but some live in the sea.

Friendly budgerigar

This helpless budgerigar chick will soon grow a colorful set of feathers. The smallest members of the parrot family, budgerigars are very social birds that live in large flocks. They huddle together for warmth and clean each other's feathers.

Stinging scorpion

A scorpion carries its young on its back. The body of this small invertebrate is protected by a hard outer skin like a suit of armor. Scorpions have eight legs and a powerful pair of pincers for grabbing prey. Arched over its back, a scorpion carries a long tail, tipped with a thorny stinging spine. The sting is used for self-defense and to kill prey.

Racing bird

The world's largest bird – the African ostrich – is taller than most humans. Although unable to fly, it can run at speeds of up to 32 mph (50 kmh) to escape enemies. Ostriches feed on vegetation, insects, small lizards, and tortoises.

Far-reaching fish

This strange-looking ray is one of the 25,000 different species of fish found worldwide. Fish populate all the world's oceans, from icy seas to warm tropical waters. Some live in freshwater rivers, lakes, pools, and underground streams. They breathe through a pair of gills that absorb oxygen from the water. Fish feed on plants and other creatures, moving through the water.

Vegetarian goat

Goats are hoofed, plant-eating mammals, which are related to the cattle family. In the wild, goats live in small groups mainly in cold, mountainous places. Domesticated (working) goats provide humans with milk, meat, and wool.

Wet-skinned toad

A member of the amphibian family, toads are related to frogs, salamanders, and newts. All amphibians have moist skin. Some live entirely in water. Most, however, live mainly on land, and only return to water to breed. Amphibians usually lay jelly-covered eggs, or spawn, but some give birth to live young.

Skin deep

Animal coats come in all forms and colors. Each type is adapted to help the animal survive by protecting it from predators and extreme weather. Fur, feathers, hair, or blubber help to keep out the cold. Spots and stripes provide camouflage, hiding the owner from enemies. Sharp spikes and tough shells form an invincible armor. Bright colors on some animals are designed to attract a mate, on others they warn predators to stay away.

Hairy pigs
Pigs may appear bald, but in fact have a layer of hair to keep heat in. These hoofed mammals have short legs, stocky bodies, and large heads. Pigs also have a long snout tipped with a flat nose with large nostrils. Their keen sense of smell helps them find food buried in the ground.

Blubbery seals
A seal's skin is covered with waterproof hair, which also protects it from injury when shuffling over rough rocks or sand. A thick layer of blubber (fat) under the skin helps to keep the seal warm – even in the coldest polar seas. The blubber also helps the seals to remain buoyant in the water.

Striped tiger
A tiger's black stripes provide excellent camouflage while it hunts in the shadowy forests of India and Indonesia. The stripes allow a tiger to sneak up on its prey before pouncing and attacking it with its sharp teeth and claws. A rare species of tiger – the white tiger – has chalky fur and stripes that are darker than usual.

Fur-coated cat
Apart from some specially bred domestic cats, kittens (baby cats) are born with a coat of fur. They will remain furry into adulthood. Fur helps to keep cats warm in the wild, especially in cold climates. When the temperature rises, a cat licks its fur to lower its body heat.

Pretty parrot
Believe it or not, this baby parrot will soon grow into one of the most brightly colored of all birds. A parrot hatchling emerges naked, blind, and helpless. After about a week, it grows a thin covering of fluffy gray feathers. Its first real feathers sprout after about one month.

Thick-skinned elephant
The largest of land animals, elephants have thick, gray, almost hairless skin. Young elephant calves are born with a coat of fine hair, which gradually falls out. The close-knit herd members all help to raise the young.

ON THE FARM

Piglets

Calf

Baby rabbits

Puppies

Gosling

Donkey foal

Baby mice

Hen and chicks

Kittens with mother

Fawn (young deer)

Fox cubs

Duckling

Lamb

Horse foal

Kitten

Kid (young goat)

Calf

IN THE WATER

Young crocodile

One-month-old spotted ray

Baby trout with yolk sack

Young toad

Young caiman

Young viperine water snake

Turtle

Seal pups

Baby seahorse

Penguin chick

Baby dogfish

Baby mole salamander

Baby Chinese turtle

Baby brown rat

Steller sea lion with young

Tiger salamander larva

WITH WINGS

Cygnet
(young swan)

Cygnet
hatching

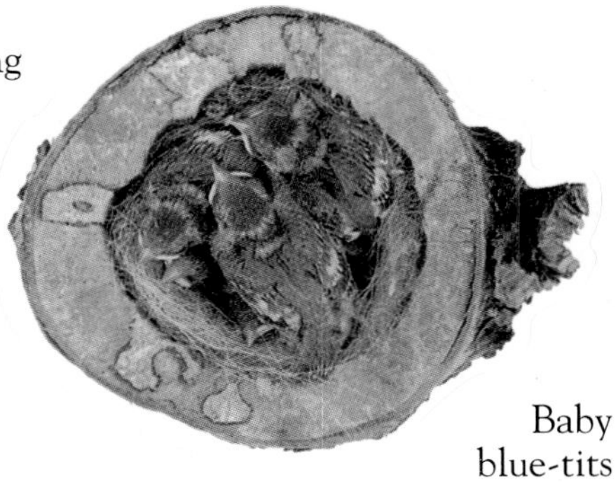

Tawny
owl chick

Baby
blue-tits

One-week-old
parrot

Moorhen chicks

Eagle
chicks

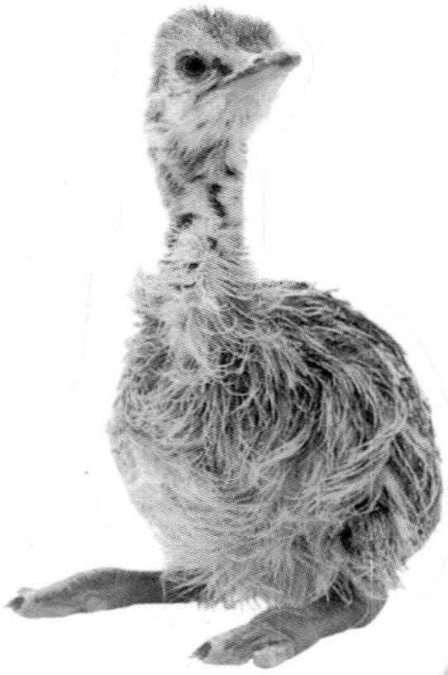

Hen chicks

Ostrich chick

Ducklings

Chaffinch
chicks

Yellow
duckling

21-day-old
budgerigar

Gosling

Penguin
chick

ON SAFARI

Young gorilla

Scorpion carrying its young

White tiger cub

Snake hatching

Leopard cub

Mother orangutan with baby

Young crocodile

Ostrich chick

Giraffe calf

Young rhinoceros

Young wallaby

Zebra foal

Young chimpanzee

Elephant calf

Baby orangutan

Lion cub

Downy gosling
Baby geese are called goslings. They have a thick layer of soft downy feathers to keep them warm until their adult feathers appear. Within a few hours of hatching from their eggs, they are able to walk, swim, and find their own food. Domestic geese are reared for their eggs, but also make good house guards – they will cry out loudly if they detect intruders.

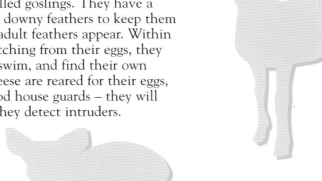

Spotted fawn
This fawn (baby deer) has a spotted coat to camouflage it from predators. Fawns stay hidden in dense undergrowth for the first few weeks after birth. They only appear to drink milk from their mother whenever she visits.

Woolly sheep
Domestic sheep provide humans with wool, meat, and milk. These sheep have a much thicker coat – called a fleece – than wild sheep. They do not shed their winter coat naturally in the spring as wild sheep do, so they have to be sheared.

Follow the zebra
Scientists are not sure why zebras have striped coats. Perhaps the stripes confuse predators or provide camouflage, or maybe they help herd members recognize each other. There are three types of zebra, each with a different pattern on its behind. These markings help zebras to follow fellow herd members when on the move.

Skin-shedding snake
Like all other reptiles, snakes have dry, scaly skin and a bony skeleton. A reptile's outer layer of skin is made mostly of a horny substance called keratin – like our fingernails. Now and then, snakes shed their skin in one piece. This lets them renew old skin and allows their bodies to grow.

Flat-shelled turtle
Turtles, along with tortoises and terrapins, are the only reptiles whose bodies are protected by hard outer shells. The shells shelter them from bad weather and attack by predators, but make moving around difficult. A turtle's shell is flat to reduce water resistance, making swimming easier.

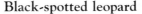

Scaly-skinned crocodile
The fierce, meat-eating crocodile has thick, scaly skin to protect it from sunburn and attack. Crocodiles control their body temperature by wading into water to cool down or basking on land to warm up. The scales are waterproof to prevent the crocodile's body from drying out.

Black-spotted leopard
The leopard's beautiful spotted coat can vary in color from yellow to gray. The black spots camouflage it as it hunts for prey. In forests, the coat is darker with more spots to help it hide in the shadows. Leopards often relax under shady rocks or on branches high in the trees.

Animal homes

Animals build a wide variety of homes to protect themselves and their young from enemies and extremes of weather. Some animals dig underground burrows or build nests high up in trees. Others spend their lives swimming in the world's oceans, rivers, and lakes. A few animals even choose to take up residence alongside humans.

Land and water
Like frogs and toads, salamanders are amphibians. This means that they are equally at home in water or on land. So while many species of salamander live in water all the time, others survive entirely on land. Some salamanders even prefer the dark, damp conditions of caves. Most salamanders, whether land- or water-based, breed in the water.

Solitary orangutan
The largest tree-dwelling animals in the world, orangutans live in the rainforests of Borneo and Sumatra. These red-haired apes live alone, although mothers look after their babies for about eight years. They choose an area of the forest that has just enough food for them to survive on. If they lived in groups or pairs, there would not be enough food to go around.

Nesting chimpanzee
Chimpanzees live in communities of between 30 and 70 individuals, which travel in smaller groups of about four to eight chimpanzees. Chimps feed and sleep in trees, but travel around their forest home, mainly on the ground, following a network of paths. At night, the chimpanzee makes a nest high up in the trees to hide from enemies.

Freshwater swan
This bedraggled little cygnet (baby swan) will grow into an elegant white adult. Swans live mostly in freshwater. They use their long necks to feed on plant stems and roots growing on the lake or river bed.

Burrowing rabbits
Rabbits prefer grassy areas with shrubs and trees, which have soft soil in which to dig. They build underground burrows to provide shelter and protection during the day, but come out at dusk to feed through the night.

Ocean home
Sea lions breed and rest on land, but are most at home in the sea. They prefer cool ocean waters, which are a good source of fish and squid, their main diet.

Forest dwellers
Gorillas live only in the lush, wet forests of west and central Africa. The forests where lowland gorillas live are warm and tropical, but mountain gorillas live in much colder forests. Every night, gorillas over the age of four make a fresh nest of dried grasses and leaves in which to sleep. During the daytime, they make a smaller nest to rest after feeding, or shelter from the rain.

Migrating trout
Trout are strong, lean fish that spend most of their lives in the sea, but migrate (travel) to rivers and streams to breed. They may swim thousands of miles until they reach a particular river. They can locate a stream by smelling tiny changes in the chemical make-up of the water.

Water snake
This viperine water snake swims across the surface of rivers by wriggling its body from side to side in S-shapes. Water snakes live in rivers, ponds, marshes, and swamps, as well as in the sea. Sea snakes live mainly in the warm waters of the Pacific and Indian Oceans where they can keep their bodies warm. They are among the most poisonous snakes in the world.

Versatile foxes
There are 21 varieties of fox, found in all types of habitat, from hot deserts to forests and the Arctic. Some live in small family groups, but most hunt for food on their own. One kind – the red fox – lives in cities and searches for food in people's garbage cans.

Hunting high and low
Eagles are found worldwide, except in the Antarctic and New Zealand. They live in varied habitats including mountains, moorlands, grasslands, deserts, marshes, seacoasts, fresh waters, and woods. Eagles perch on cliff tops or treetops, and use their telescopic vision to spot distant prey before swooping in for the kill.

City lovers
Brown rats never live far away from humans. They like buildings and, since they are good swimmers, are often found in underground sewers. They cause much damage by raiding human food supplies and chewing through pipes and cables.

Water world
This turtle prefers the fresh waters of rivers, but most turtles spend their lives swimming through the tropical oceans of the world. Some turtles migrate great distances between feeding sites and beaches where they lay their eggs.

Early days

Some animals, such as seahorses, are born as fully formed tiny versions of adults. Others, such as blue-tit hatchlings, are quite undeveloped and helpless at birth. Whatever their start in life, baby animals are at risk from changes in the weather, a lack of food, and predators. Many young animals are left to fend for themselves as soon as they are born, others are fed and protected by their parents until they are able to look after themselves.

Home-alone penguins

When penguin chicks are only two or three weeks old, their parents swim off to sea to find food. The chicks are left to huddle together for warmth. They are unable to enter the water until they have grown waterproof adult feathers.

Begging blue-tits

Blue-tit nestlings are completely helpless and depend totally on their parents for the first few weeks of life. Fed mainly on caterpillars, they grow rapidly. After learning to fly, they still beg food from their parents for several days, until they learn to fend for themselves.

Independent chicks

As soon as they hatch, baby hens (chicks) follow the first moving object they see – usually the mother hen. Within a few hours of hatching, chicks can run around and find food. However, if a chick takes food before an adult, it is punished with a sharp peck.

A rough start

Four out of five lion cubs die before they are two years old. While adult lions go off to hunt, the young are at risk from hyenas and other lions. Cubs are not skilled at fighting for food, so many starve to death. If a male lion takes over a pride (family), he will kill the cubs.

Crying out loud

Baby owls (chicks) grow a thick layer of soft down to keep them warm. Owl chicks need a steady supply of food, such as mice, so they make loud calls to let their parents know they are hungry.

Swimming seahorses

Instead of the mother seahorse having babies inside her body, it is the male who carries the growing young around. The female seahorse lays her eggs into a pouch on her partner's belly. It takes just over one month for the babies to develop and hatch. The wall of the male's pouch breaks and perfectly formed miniature seahorses swim out.

Pouch protection

When a wallaby is born, it is tiny and furless. It grows inside a pouch on its mother's stomach. After a few months, the young wallaby comes out for short periods of time. It returns to suckle, sleep, and escape danger. After nine months, it is too big for the pouch but still sticks its head inside to feed.